Self-Esteem

Comprehensive Manual For Individuals Of All Genders
And Age Groups, Offering Valuable Insights On
Cultivating Self-esteem And Confidence

Vincent Douglas

TABLE OF CONTENT

What Is Your Self-Perception?...................................1

The Dichotomy Of Self-Esteem And Self-Confidence..4

Develop Awareness Of Your Unfavorable Behaviors..20

How To Identify Acquaintances With The Potential For Friendship...32

Enrich Your Personal Well-Being Through Acts Of Kindness..46

The Psychological Benefits Of Setting Goals....51

The Fairness Experiment..59

Effective Practices To Cultivate A Positive Self-Image..68

Choosing The Right Company................................82

Superlative Methods To Enhance Your Optimism..101

Regulating Key Emotions...................................... 106

The Benefits Associated With Possessing Self-Assurance..113

What Is Your Self-Perception?

The recurring statement, 'It is a world predominantly for men,' tends to have a profound impact on numerous individuals of the male gender, particularly those who struggle with their self-assurance and sense of worth. Even after the widespread acceptance of gender equality, the male population is still expected to fulfill numerous responsibilities in every aspect of our lives. Men are consistently held to high standards of performance, whether it be in the realms of business, sports, entertainment, or any other field. This implicit anticipation that is communicated non-verbally challenges men to engage in competitiveness, and the principle of "survival of the fittest" continues to prevail as the prevailing standard.

This presents a significant obstacle for individuals of the male gender who suffer from feelings of insecurity and an absence of self-confidence and self-worth, which hinder their ability to fully exploit their capabilities. Many individuals, despite the pressures and expectations imposed by society, are capable of venturing into the world and openly demonstrating their preparedness to achieve great success. This is not due to a lack of talent or abilities, but rather stems from their diminished self-esteem and inadequate self-confidence.

Can an authentic distinction be identified between the two? Are there any methods or strategies for enhancing one or both of these aspects?

The objective of this eBook is to furnish you with a coherent comprehension of the principles surrounding self-esteem and self-confidence. It is designed to assist you in surmounting any obstacles that may impede your progress towards achieving your goals and fulfilling your potential, thereby enabling you to rightfully assert your position in society.

It is our hope that after reading this book, you will have enough information for you to conquer your shyness, inhibitions, and other obstacles that prevent you from being the best that you can.

The Dichotomy Of Self-Esteem And Self-Confidence

Many individuals conflate the concepts of self-esteem and self-confidence. Indeed, when individuals engage in discussions concerning confidence, they are often referring to self-esteem and vice versa. It is quite common for numerous individuals to hold the misconception that self-esteem and confidence are indistinguishable. No, they're not. They are two entirely distinct entities. They do exert influence on oneself; that is a common aspect they share. However, in their mode of operation, impact, and application, they diverge significantly.

It is of utmost importance to grasp the distinction between self-esteem and self-confidence, even though they are interrelated. By acquiring an understanding of how these two concepts manifest in your personal experiences, you can subsequently construct an effective framework that will empower you to lead a more confident and fulfilled life. That is our primary objective. However, before we can attain that objective, it is imperative that we take measures to confront and rectify issues concerning self-esteem.

What is Self-Esteem?

Self-esteem refers to the assessment one makes of their own worth. You observe your own reflection, prompting a variety of assessments and evaluations. You develop a narrative or personal account pertaining to your intrinsic worth as an individual, your position within society, and your significance. Can one make sacrifices for your benefit? Do you merit an abundance of anything? How important are you? These queries pertain to one's self-worth. These questions pertain to principles regarding personal worth, wherein you assign significance to your own being.

What is self-confidence? Self-assurance can be understood as the outward manifestation of the inherent value, standing, significance, and efficacy that one perceives within oneself. While self-esteem predominantly resides within the individual, operating discreetly in a realm of civil discourse and personal introspection that eludes most observers, self-confidence manifests itself prominently in the external sphere.

Allow me to rephrase that using a more formal tone: "Allow me to illustrate the idea in this manner: if one harbors the perception of being a profound disappointment, it is likely that one's behavior will reflect a predisposition towards failure." You commence exerting yourself in a manner reflective of someone who lacks inherent worth, an individual who fails to exhibit self-regard.

Self-assurance constitutes the manner in which individuals communicate signals to the external world, shaping its perception and appraisal of their identity and worth. As it may be discernible, there exists a close association between self-confidence and self-esteem, as they emanate from a shared origin. While one is purely internal, the other is external and public. This is the factor that gives rise to ambiguity. Many individuals hold the belief that both things are indistinguishable. While originating from a common source, it should be noted that self-esteem is exclusively derived internally.

Now, from this perspective, it is possible for individuals to perceive you as a person who has achieved success. One may be under the impression that you possess considerable wealth, influence, and remarkable qualities. All of these are evaluations from external sources. Nevertheless, if one holds the belief that they possess no value and are no more than an insignificant pile of refuse, it is unlikely that any form of external validation will be effective in alleviating their underlying self-esteem problems. Self-esteem, indeed, pertains to an intrinsic assessment of one's own worth, aligning with an individual's personal narrative encompassing their value, position in society, significance, and importance.

Self-esteem can be described as an intrinsic sense of self-assurance.

To avoid any potential confusion, allow me to provide a concise elucidation of self-esteem: it encompasses the internalized sense of self-assurance. You perceive your intrinsic worth as an individual and hold the conviction that you possess inherent value. You can do it. You possess the necessary qualities; you are indeed a rightful member, and so forth. It pertains merely to the internalization of one's inherent ability and the subjective worth one assigns to oneself.

Nevertheless, it is crucial to highlight that self-esteem ultimately stems from personal appraisal. It exhibits a sense of intimacy; it is internalized. You prioritize your inherent value and prioritize the recognition of your self-worth.

The Extrinsic Factors of Self-Assurance

If self-esteem becomes ingrained within one's self-assurance, then self-assurance manifests as the outward projection of one's self-esteem. Presently, I hesitate to cause any misunderstanding, however, considering that the foundation of your character lies in the choices you make regarding your self-worth or self-esteem, it logically follows that your actions in the external world are a manifestation or expression of your internal state. To put it differently, the starting point lies in the realm of your self-esteem and the beliefs you consciously adopt pertaining to your own identity. It commences with the narrative you construct pertaining to your position in the world, your worth, your significance, and your potential. Nevertheless, it continues to advance and resolves itself.

What is the apparent manifestation of this, in terms of its objective outcome? What perspective does the global community hold? The external world would gather distinct indications. It would be advantageous to take heed of your nonverbal cues. Do you present yourself in such a manner that others perceive you as self-assured in your capability to accomplish tasks? Alternatively, wouldn't it be preferable for you to feel confident that you possess a thorough understanding of the subject matter, if not more? Do your nonverbal cues align with this statement?

Individuals would also give consideration to your facial expressions. Do you find it challenging to maintain direct eye contact with others? Do you consistently experience the need to avert your gaze due to feelings of embarrassment? Do you encounter difficulties in effectively conveying specific expressions? Additionally, these are subject to interpretation due to the fact that individuals who possess confidence often exhibit distinct facial expressions. They do not seek to exert dominance over others; they do not intend to forcefully impose their self-assured nature onto others. Conversely, their faith is inherent. It instills a sense of tranquility in individuals, while concurrently exhibiting a perceptible aura of inner stability.

Moreover, the display of self-assurance is evident in our approach to circumstances. In situations involving potential embarrassment or the potential for conflict, do you tend to instinctively retreat or promptly offer an apology? Does your intuition promptly assume responsibility and attempt to conceal any errors, with the expectation that others will not observe your mistake? The manner in which you navigate situations greatly influences the degree to which individuals perceive you as credible.

If one possesses a proactive nature, individuals tend to take notice and acknowledge such rare qualities due to their scarcity. Most people are passive. The manner in which you manage situations is significantly influenced by the extent of your self-assurance.

The selection of your words serves as an indication of your level of confidence. It is a common occurrence for individuals not to express themselves by saying, "I do not possess any financial resources." It is an unattainable feat. They inquire, "In what manner may I accomplish that?" "By what means can I generate the necessary funds?" In alternative phrasing, individuals inquire about the methods or strategies available to them in order to achieve their desired financial outcome.

Contrast this with statements that demonstrate disregard, such as affirming, "I am currently unable to afford it." I'm broke. It is improbable for that event to transpire." With which individual would you prefer to socialize? I thought so.

Ultimately, another external aspect pertaining to self-assurance pertains to one's manner of speech. If you belong to the category of individuals who struggle to communicate assertively and project confidence in their abilities due to a lack of vocal projection, it could potentially pose a concern. Individuals will not seek your counsel for solutions. Individuals will not seek your guidance for the purpose of obtaining inspiration. How can you effectively address their needs and preferences when it is evident that you possess a limited understanding of the subject matter? Alternatively, do you not convey indications that you possess a conviction and assurance in the correctness of your statements and beliefs?

What level of significance do these external indicators hold in terms of one's self-assurance? These entities hold significance due to their capacity to generate effects on others. It is essential to bear in mind that one's self-confidence should not be attributed to a lack of alternative engagements or pursuits. Self-confidence should not be regarded as a mere superficial marker or embellishment. It is not akin to a vibrant jacket that one dons, which attracts attention and garners compliments. Instead, it possesses a profound impact on those in one's vicinity. When such an effect occurs, it subsequently accumulates to alter your role.

How does this scenario unfold? When you project outward signals of confidence, you exert an influence on others that engenders trust. They experience an increased level of comfort; they perceive a greater sense of familiarity. They display a greater disposition towards assisting others, and consequently, these characteristics contribute to the cultivation of increasingly elevated levels of esteem. These factors also foster the perception that you are intricately affiliated with their team, they are equally involved in your team, and a genuine bond exists between you.

Stated differently, the state of being self-assured empowers individuals to effect favorable transformations within their environment and immediate circumstances. The importance of self-confidence cannot be overstated, for it is crucial to note that the world at large is unconcerned with one's personal emotions. Indeed, one may experience a sense of great potency, yet it holds true only if that inner strength translates into tangible deeds. Engaging in such activities may not yield fruitful results, as societal recognition is often reserved for meaningful contributions.

One means by which one is capable of effectuating change is by exerting a significant influence or instilling sufficient inspiration in others, thereby eliciting altered behaviors or actions on their part. Can you comprehend the functioning of this system? That's the criteria by which the world assesses individuals. That is the manner in which society evaluates individuals. This matter is entirely objective, as the focus lies solely on outcomes. All this discourse concerning emotions, sentiments, hypothetical scenarios, intentions, or perceived intentions is utterly nonsensical.

None of that matters. What carries significance in the realm of the world is solely determined by one's actions. What measures did you take to alter your immediate environment? To what extent did you influence individuals in your vicinity? Have individuals ceased exhibiting altered conduct? To clarify, the global perspective encompasses the study of interpersonal relationships and the intricate dynamics that give rise to cascading sequences of behaviors. Put simply, this is evident. This is not hypothetical; this is not conjecture. You either engaged in an action, or you refrained from doing so. You have either exerted influence, or you have not.

That's how vital self-confidence is because, on an objective level, it changes your reality. When exerting influence upon individuals, it may prompt a shift in their behavior, thereby fostering collective progress towards a shared objective. It is within your capability to initiate interactions that facilitate targeted transformations. It is important to note that these modifications can have both advantageous and disadvantageous implications. That's not the point. The essence lies in the fact that the world assesses individuals solely on the outcomes they generate. This can yield both favorable outcomes, as well as detrimental outcomes.

Develop Awareness Of Your Unfavorable Behaviors

Undesirable behaviors manifest through one's nonverbal communication. If one possesses lazy tendencies, they tend to exhibit a significant amount of slouching. Individuals who engage in deceptive behavior often exhibit a higher frequency of blinking compared to their counterparts. Various inferences can be drawn from one's body language, and if one desires to exude confidence, it is imperative to recognize and address any adverse habits, as these behaviors fail to foster a favorable impression among others.

Do you have the habit of biting your nails?

If you engage in such behavior, it will be readily observed by others. Such aspects are especially discernible to those who conduct the interview process. It is quite apparent that you lack self-assurance. It is strongly recommended that you consider undergoing a treatment to address this behavior, as it can significantly contribute to improving your self-perception. Habits are formed solely as a result of consistent repetition. Accordingly, on each occasion when you feel inclined to bring your hand towards your mouth, redirect your actions towards an alternative activity that remains consistent, ultimately facilitating the substitution of your habit. Each instance in which you submit to it serves to further solidify the behavior. Nevertheless, in the event that you conceive an alternative course of action, compel yourself to execute it. As an illustration, in the event that you discover yourself inclining towards placing your hand near your mouth with the intention of biting your nails, I suggest grasping a pencil and jotting down a specific objective to be accomplished today. That is an excellent practice to substitute your unfavorable behavior. Upon observing the growth of your nails and acknowledging their need for a manicure, a sense of satisfaction will be experienced.

You indulge in excessive smoking.

Initially, smoking can be commonly observed as a behavioral pattern adopted within social contexts. Nevertheless, in current times, there exists little justification for exhibiting such conspicuous smoking behavior. Indulging in consecutive smoking sessions reveals to those in your vicinity that you possess an anxious temperament. Might I suggest considering the purchase of a pack of nicotine patches or nicotine chewing gums, as they can effectively serve as substitutes for the nicotine intake typically obtained through smoking cigarettes? The condition of your body is directly proportional to the care and attention it receives. Every cigarette that you smoke gives you bad body image, but it is also leading to killing you bit by bit. Take pride in the fact that you utilize alternatives. You will incur the displeasure of a smaller number of individuals and emit a more pleasant scent.

When experiencing tension or unease, individuals often resort to engaging their hands in physical movements.

When navigating within a space, endeavor to maintain your hands at your sides. When you take a seat, endeavor to emulate the same action. If you are aware that you engage in the excessive movement of your fingers, overcome this habit by placing your hands discreetly beneath your legs.

Focus on cultivating behaviors and mannerisms that demonstrate a lack of self-assurance. Enumerated below are a few examples of such instances which will aid in your identification of them should they occur. It typically requires a duration of approximately 31 days to develop a commendable routine. Therefore, upon the observation of the resurgence of the former habit, it is advisable to substitute it with a more positive habit, as such action will contribute significantly towards the enhancement of one's self-assurance.

- Averting one's gaze when engaging in conversation

- Gazing downwards with an attitude of submissiveness ● Casting one's eyes downwards in a submissive manner ● Directing one's gaze downwards in a humble fashion ● Lowering one's gaze in a submissive gesture

- Involuntarily applying pressure to your lip with your teeth

- Moistening your lips using your tongue

- Failing to remain motionless ● Being constantly in motion ● Not maintaining a static position

- Demonstrating excessive concern over conveying one's message

- Exhibiting dependency and seeking confirmation
- Displaying a need for validation and seeking reassurance
- Demonstrating reliance and seeking approval

Allow us to examine several of these matters as they hold significant relevance and influence on the perception individuals form while observing your actions in such undertakings. If one averts their gaze from individuals while being addressed, it conveys a variety of impressions. It appears that you may either possess a lack of interest in hearing their perspective, or alternatively, have an inclination to swiftly disengage from the ongoing discourse. To optimize your conversational experience, it is recommended that you maintain direct eye contact with the speaker without engaging in excessive blinking. Look interested. Please appear attentive.

By assuming a posture of submissively gazing downward, one inadvertently exposes oneself to potential exploitation by others. The rationale behind this is that a specific demographic derives exhilaration from wielding authority, despite being cognizant of the inherent limitations thereof. Take bullies for instance. They derive pleasure from inflicting pain upon those who exhibit vulnerability. Should you persist in projecting a submissive demeanor, you inadvertently draw individuals of this disposition into your life. Therefore, rather than appearing submissive, it is advisable to practice maintaining an upright posture. Maintain direct eye contact and refrain from retreating when engaging in conversation with others.

The inclination to constantly seek affirmation and validation is an undesirable trait. How frequently have you conveyed this message to your supervisor?

Are you satisfied with the advancements I made today?

"Is there anything wrong with my performance?

Do you believe there exists a possibility for me to comprehend this in the future?

The employment of your conventional expressions aimed at garnering admiration works to your disadvantage.

These behaviors indicate a deficiency in self-assurance and can cause fatigue among those around you, as they prefer to collaborate with individuals who possess the composure and autonomy to proceed with their tasks without relying on external validation. It is not frequently observed that managers and CEOs request such authorization. They possess the knowledge of proper conduct. If one discovers oneself engaging in such behavior, one should promptly begin to modify the expressions employed as a means to manifest one's assurance and credibility pertaining to the entrusted responsibility. When your supervisor assigns you a task, respond:

"No problem. I will attend to that matter promptly."

"Thanks a lot. I would be grateful to know the tasks assigned to me for today.

May I seek assistance from someone for this undertaking?

Having a comprehensive skill set is not a requirement, although submissiveness should never be a characteristic displayed. Be happy. Strive to embody the qualities and characteristics that you would appreciate in a professional colleague. Please be aware that within a professional setting, one must acknowledge the limitations of time in completing tasks. If one anticipates constant accolades from their employer, such expectations rarely align with reality. Should such an occurrence transpire, it can be attributed to an excessive display of dependence on your part. Effortlessly fulfill your responsibilities with genuine dedication, and in the event that you encounter unfamiliar tasks, seek elucidation through inquiring. Maintain a cordial demeanor towards your colleagues and refrain from allowing personal matters to infiltrate the professional environment. It is important to bear in mind that they might be facing as well their own challenges, and by exuding a sense of happiness, you contribute to brightening their days.

How To Identify Acquaintances With The Potential For Friendship

Individuals possess an inherent aversion towards feelings of solitude, and once they perceive that engaging in a basic conversation with another person could alleviate their sense of isolation, they are likely to do so. Many individuals who experience shyness often perceive a sense of solitude as they struggle to muster the confidence to engage in conversation with others, even when they are physically in close proximity. Nevertheless, it is crucial to acknowledge the existence of particular societal norms that can induce feelings of unease. These norms often create an apprehension that interacting with others is challenging and that maintaining one's personal space ensures a sense of security. In view of these circumstances, it is worth noting that many individuals who exhibit shyness have experienced instances in which they have been disappointed by others. Consequently, harboring feelings of apprehension in the presence of unfamiliar individuals can be perceived as a protective measure for one's own well-being.

Strangers

Isolation can have detrimental effects on certain individuals, instilling feelings of inadequacy and unpreparedness for the challenges of life. In the case of introverted children starting school, they are suddenly thrust into social situations that may surpass what they have encountered before, akin to engaging in a conflict with only a weapon but lacking the necessary firepower. Certain children may develop a tendency towards shy behavior characterized by cynicism. Put another way, individuals might experience such a profound sense of detachment from society that it leads to animosity towards their peers. In a societal context where there is a prevailing inclination towards establishing connections, experiencing exclusion can evoke profound frustration. Many introverted individuals make concerted efforts to establish connections with their peers, disproving the misconception that shyness is synonymous with being passive. Individuals who exhibit shyness experience a sense of enthusiasm upon receiving invitations to social gatherings. To their dismay, however, they often encounter feelings of despondency caused by their belief that they are ill-prepared. This sentiment stems from their inability to gather the confidence required to initiate conversations. Certain individuals endeavor to find the bravery to establish connections by diminishing their inhibitions via the consumption of alcoholic beverages and substances, a course of action that offers only momentary relief, and moreover, carries the potential for grave consequences.

Individuals are urged to engage in interpersonal communication as a means of preempting sentiments of hostility and resentment towards fellow members of social collectives. Ultimately, individuals seek a sense of inclusion and validation, along with an assurance that the world fosters a secure environment.

friends

Following the initial introductions and brief exchange of commonplace conversation, it becomes imperative to devise strategies that set you apart from individuals who, initially, may appear somewhat similar.

If your prospective acquaintances do not acquire any unique knowledge about you, either due to your inherent reticence or conversations that fail to move beyond banal subjects, it is improbable that you will establish a profound rapport with them. It would be inherently difficult for them to discern the presence of any meaningful commonalities between the two of you that might warrant further exploration, or any mutually shared interests that could potentially serve as the basis for engaging in more profound discussions at some point in the future. They will possess no knowledge of your capabilities, limitations, idiosyncrasies, and allure. Certainly, this is scarcely knowledge that necessitates public disclosure to just anyone, and certain characteristics may indeed be more suitable for concealment until a genuine sense of closeness is established.

Nevertheless, the act of divulging specific pieces of information that could be intriguing serves to foster and enhance new friendships by offering insights into one's own self. Consequently, your newfound associates will be more prone to reciprocate, potentially divulging common idiosyncrasies, pursuits, or habits that you can mutually relish and elaborate upon.

Frequently, the primary impediment to allowing others to catch glimpses of our personality and interests stems from a sense of embarrassment. What if they have a negative reception of those attributes or preferences, leading to our own personal humiliation? What if they perceive the information we disclose as inappropriate or overly direct, leading to a perpetual state of discomfort and estrangement between them and us? Frequently, we often deceive ourselves by assuming that our preferences and individual traits will not be amicable to others. However, the only means to ascertain this is by openly sharing these aspects with potential acquaintances. Concealing those aspects would result in a lack of vibrancy, as none of your most commendable personal traits or enjoyable hobbies would be displayed whatsoever. In addition, by doing so, you will circumvent the possibility of discovering whether they derive satisfaction from comparable pursuits or possess idiosyncrasies that align with your own. This would be regrettable as common hobbies and traits serve as unequivocal catalysts for fostering a connection and leaving a lasting impact.

In regards to the methodology for achieving this objective, it can be considered relatively uncomplicated. In the event that something arises which captivates or enthuses you, kindly bring it to our attention. Inquire of your associate for their perspective and subsequently ascertain your own. In this way, you can discuss skills, hobbies, even qualities you possess or value in others in a relatively organic way. Exercise caution to avoid imposing your perspectives upon your conversational partner. Convey your thoughts with fervor, while maintaining an objective and impartial approach. You may uncover numerous shared interests, however, conversely, the opposite outcome is also plausible. In the event that you realize you share limited commonalities with an individual who was previously unknown to you, it would be of little benefit to sever ties or foster animosity. If you encounter a situation where your viewpoints diverge considerably to a degree that makes it difficult to continue in a cordial manner, it would be advisable to transition to a different subject or, if necessary, gracefully conclude the conversation. In the event that an individual occasionally espouses divergent values or appears to exhibit no common interests, refrain from interpreting it as a personal affront. In numerous instances, when one adopts a versatile approach and demonstrates genuine curiosity, it is possible to discover unexpected areas of similarity or, at the very least, gain a thought-provoking new vantage point. In the end, it is improbable that any negative consequences will arise from exhibiting your personal interests and traits. The most unfavorable outcome would result in both individuals parting ways, with their respective mentalities remaining unaffected. In alternative situations, it is possible that you could derive satisfaction from engaging in dialogue with individuals who possess contrasting perspectives to yours, provided that you acquire comprehension of the underlying rationale behind their viewpoints. Do not permit apprehensions of embarrassment, criticism, or alienation impede you from revealing your authentic self to others. Engaging in valid and legitimate conversations with others can only be achieved through this method, and the potential risks associated with it are relatively insignificant, making it worthwhile.

Colleagues

In the event of fortuitously encountering a friend, colleague, or acquaintance from one's distant past, it is deemed permissible to adopt a less formal demeanor. Even a brief salutation such as, "Greetings! How are you? It has been a considerable duration since we last interacted, and acknowledging this fact would likely initiate the conversation, potentially even contributing to an extended dialogue or the possibility of future interactions. Nonetheless, it is advisable to familiarize oneself with these guidelines in order to maximize the potential for a fortuitous encounter to yield fruitful and harmonious outcomes.

Please demonstrate your keen interest and enthusiasm towards the upcoming meeting. One can express the same sentiment in a more formal tone by saying, "It has been an extended period of time since last we met. How have you been?" or "I am pleased to encounter you once more after a considerable absence. What has transpired in your life?"

Remember to maintain a pleasant facial expression and establish visual contact by meeting the other person's gaze. Based on your previous association, you have the option to engage in either a handshake or an embrace as an expression of greeting, recognizing that physical contact is not obligatory in every circumstance.

Engage in active listening to the information conveyed by your acquaintance, while also providing your own pertinent personal details. However, it would be advisable to provide a concise account as there is minimal necessity to delve into the intricate particulars of your personal experiences. Inquire about other individuals within the family, if you possess knowledge regarding their identities, as this conveys your genuine interest and prolongs the discourse.

If you are not at ease, there is no obligation for you to divulge specific information. Merely express, "Nothing extraordinary, merely adhering to the customary routine of work, study, and home." Alternatively, you could respond with, "The routine remains unchanged, no notable deviations." However, if the other person kindly shared a snippet of information about their own life, you might still need to provide a bit more elaboration.

Conclude the casual conversation by extending an invitation for a prospective engagement at a later point in time, with the possibility of uncertainty. One may express the same sentiment by stating, "One could propose, 'Shall we arrange a meeting at a suitable time to enjoy a coffee together?' without necessarily seeking or offering contact information, unless specifically requested." You may provide either your social media account, cellphone number, or email address, according to your current preference.

Enrich Your Personal Well-Being Through Acts Of Kindness

In order to circumvent emotional manipulation, it is necessary to cultivate proficiency in impartial thinking. Neutral thinking is distinct as it operates in contrast to the propensity of becoming entangled in a myriad of experiences and thoughts. Cultivating impartiality towards oneself may require some effort and discipline. Once you acquire the skill of objective thinking, you will begin to discern your thoughts, emotions, and actions without adopting a critical stance. This will undoubtedly assist you in your pursuit of self-discovery.

To advance as individuals, it is imperative for us to comprehend that our thoughts do not define us. Your thoughts are distinct from your identity. They do not serve as an accurate reflection of your character. They operate autonomously from your influence. Thoughts are not intentional constructs to be actively nurtured, but rather spontaneous occurrences that require adaptation and skillful navigation. It is necessary for you to assume a passive stance and observe your thoughts in a detached manner, much like watching a television program. Observe the content displayed on the television as it cycles through channels autonomously. It will traverse the path from this location to that destination, spanning the duration from the past to the future. The mind will exhibit a plethora of wandering thoughts, presenting various scenarios for contemplation. Subsequently, you have the privilege of determining what deserves your attention. You will inevitably discern the emergence of a thought. One can enhance their ability to recognize this thought by perceiving its emergence in their consciousness as if observed through a metaphorical window, gently observing its presence before allowing it to naturally dissipate and exit their stream of consciousness. This illustration facilitates the recognition that your thoughts possess an innate detachment from your authentic self and hover within the ethereal realms, yet they lack true existence. This phenomenon often goes unnoticed by the majority: thoughts hold no tangible reality.

Upon careful contemplation of its intricacy, one will come to recognize that one's thoughts embody an exceedingly abstract notion. The act involves employing language skills acquired through learning to generate immediate and self-contained verbalized thoughts within our minds. It is a subject that can provide ample opportunity for contemplation and introspection, should it pique your interest. Please take a moment to ponder the marvel of consciousness.

Consciousness fundamentally pertains to the human mind, distinct from the cognition exhibited by animals. The human form is considered to be the most extraordinary asset that we are aware of within the cosmos. The expansive capacity of the human mind has given rise to civilizations that have both excelled in remarkable goodness and unleashed horrifying malevolence. The mind cannot be measured or quantified; it exists solely in the realm of abstraction. Specific techniques are capable of measuring behavior, brain chemicals, or specific aspects of brain function. Nonetheless, it remains an inherent limitation that one can never fully comprehend the subjective experiences of another individual. They possess the capability to articulate it to you, however, as we shall deliberate upon, language serves as a rudimentary instrument and may not invariably yield precision. All of the descriptions and quantification in the world cannot account for this basic separation. The notion of division is what grants us our humanity and instigates the imperative for individuality.

The Psychological Benefits Of Setting Goals

Establishing objectives can facilitate the realization of the desired lifestyle. It has the potential to provide individuals with a sense of focus and guidance. This chapter provides an overview of the advantages that can be derived from establishing goals for enhancing one's overall well-being. It further elaborates upon how leveraging your personal attributes can aptly contribute towards facilitating the establishment and attainment of objectives.

Sorrow and positivity

Goals provide individuals with a sense of direction and anticipation. Your existence holds inherent meaning, elevating your sense of optimism and hope. Regardless of whether your objectives are of a long-term or short-term nature, you are providing yourself with a purpose to rise from slumber each morning.

The connection between hope and goal setting operates reciprocally. Contemplating and strategizing your objectives can bolster a sense of anticipation and confidence. This sense of positivity can subsequently enhance your capacity to accomplish your objectives.

It will also aid you in formulating additional objectives in the future. An individual who possesses optimism is capable of delineating their objectives, understanding the means by which they will attain them, and is driven to accomplish them. In addition, hope serves as a catalyst in aiding individuals to navigate through any intricacies and thereby maintaining perseverance in times of adversity.

Taking control

If one establishes and attains daily objectives, this will culminate in significant achievements toward overarching goals by the end of the year. And this is entirely your own creation. People of resolute determination assert authority over their lives, instead of idly meandering or surrendering their decision-making power to others. Acknowledge the sensation of dominion and self-empowerment as you establish and subsequently achieve your objectives.

Consider a scenario where you are faced with an unavoidable work deadline. Alternatively, what if you were to opt to meet that deadline in advance? Alternatively, suppose you belong to the category of individuals who frequently surpass deadlines and habitually provide excuses. In that case, it would be beneficial for you to reverse this trend and exert concentrated effort towards meeting those deadlines.

Acknowledge the extent of your capabilities. Even a change in mindset can bestow a sense of mastery. Acquiring the ability to surmount obstacles and cultivate a more positive outlook towards uncontrollable circumstances can greatly enhance one's confidence.

Flow experience

By establishing consistent and significant objectives, you position yourself to encounter a greater number of flow experiences. A flow experience entails complete absorption of one's consciousness in a specific activity.

Considerations of time and other fundamental necessities, such as hunger, are disregarded. Positive psychologists generally concur that the greater one's experiences of flow, the greater their level of happiness. Goals afford us an active engagement opportunity, which is a crucial element in fostering a state of flow.

In order to attain this condition, it is crucial to possess a distinct purpose. Evidently, establishing clear objectives serves as a commendable outset. Furthermore, it is imperative to select an objective that poses a substantial challenge, yet remains within the limits of your capabilities. If the level of difficulty is insufficient, you will inevitably experience tedium.

It is advisable to periodically reassess your goals in order to maintain motivation. Furthermore, try to obtain regular feedback so you are aware of how you are doing. Seeking assistance from others may prove to be a prudent course of action, alternatively, it is recommended to diligently monitor and evaluate one's advancements in a systematic manner.

There exists a positive correlation between goals and the experience of flow. Through the establishment of goals, we increase our likelihood of experiencing flow. By attaining a state of flow, it is more probable that we will successfully accomplish our objectives.

General wellbeing

Possessing ambitions and aims in our existence contributes to our overall wellness. It affords us with the chance to embark on a journey from which we can glean knowledge and derive pleasure. It facilitates an individual's recognition of their abilities, imparts meaning to life, and enhances optimism. In light of this, it can alleviate stress and mitigate the likelihood of experiencing depression. Engaging in goal-oriented activities enhances one's focus and contributes to an elevation in happiness levels.

Objective establishment and leveraging your capabilities

When establishing and pursuing your goals, take into account the potential utilization of your personal strengths to facilitate the attainment of your objectives. It is important to be cognizant of one's primary strengths, as these are the ones that can be employed with greater ease. Leveraging these strengths can serve as a significant source of motivation.

Take into account the ways in which the following advantageous qualities can support you in establishing your objectives:

In the pursuit of generating ideas, having a deep sense of inquisitiveness, originality, and a genuine passion for acquiring knowledge can greatly facilitate the process. This can prove beneficial when deliberating over the selection of objectives, devising strategies for their attainment, and devising approaches to address any possible obstacles.

Courage can serve as a catalyst for pursuing the ambitious aspirations that have remained unattainable thus far. This particular attribute will empower you to take action, despite any uncertainties you may have. If perseverance is the foundation of your abilities, then you are certain to accomplish the objectives you have established for yourself.

Embracing a humorous disposition as one's fortitude empowers individuals to find amusement even in adverse situations, thereby showcasing a positive and light-hearted outlook on life.

Exercising prudence enables individuals to carefully evaluate whether the objectives they currently desire align with their long-term aspirations. Remaining true to oneself while setting goals demonstrates authenticity. It guarantees that you are undertaking these actions for self-fulfillment rather than to meet the expectations of others.

An alternative way to utilize personal strengths in goal setting is by specifically establishing a goal aimed at cultivating a particular strength. For example, if you desire to improve your kindness, you may choose to engage in voluntary work at an organization dedicated to assisting others.

An alternative approach would be to utilize goal setting as a means to cultivate a specific strength, albeit the strength itself not being the primary objective. For example, your objective is to compose a novel. Nevertheless, during the course of your journey, you choose to demonstrate the power of gratitude by actively acknowledging the individuals who provided assistance in your pursuit of your objective. Regardless of the objectives you establish for yourself, derive pleasure from the journey and contemplate how they are proving advantageous to you throughout the process.

The Fairness Experiment

Have you ever observed your surroundings and pondered the existence of inequities between those who possess and those who lack? Perhaps you have experienced a sense of envy towards those who possess the ability to effortlessly articulate themselves, as your self-assurance seems to hinder your own expression. An experiment was conducted by an Italian individual named Pareto, which gave rise to the renowned principle known as the 80/20 rule. The statement indicates that in a specific region of Italy, a significant proportion of the population, namely 80 percent, display diligent work ethics, yet it is the remaining 20 percent who primarily reap the rewards. The premise at hand holds its curiosity not in its application to the dichotomy of individuals with and without material possessions. It is equally applicable to all facets of existence. Life is oftentimes perceived as unjust, causing individuals to forego the gratifying aspects of their existence due to a lack of adeptness in implementing this principle into their own lives. Allow me to demonstrate how this can positively impact your levels of self-assurance.

Enumerate areas in which you possess a high level of confidence.

One might perceive this to be inconsequential, yet it holds significant weight. You possess adeptness in handling domestic tasks. You possess the knowledge and ability to take care of your personal well-being, including maintaining oral hygiene by brushing your teeth. Perhaps you possess the knowledge and skillset required to operate a motor vehicle. We kindly request that you evaluate all the areas in which you possess expertise. Now, we need to look at the percentage of your life that you spend doing things that make you feel uncomfortable and lacking in confidence. These are moments wherein you engage in activities that do not elicit happiness or contentment, but rather persevering through them out of necessity. In order to bolster your self-esteem, it is essential to allocate a greater portion of your time towards cultivating positive thoughts about oneself. Consequently, it becomes necessary to prioritize engaging in activities that align with your strengths, rather than spending considerable amounts of time on endeavors that are not aligned with your abilities.

Let us consider the scenario wherein you allocate 20 percent of your time towards activities that do not contribute positively towards your self-esteem. Hence, it is imperative that you allocate a greater proportion of your time towards engaging in activities that bring you joy and imbue your existence with a sense of purpose and fulfillment. I would highly recommend that you allocate a greater amount of time towards engaging in the activities mentioned below. By allocating more time to engaging in activities that foster self-confidence, individuals may discover a corresponding increase in their overall sense of self-worth. If one consistently strives to increase that percentage on a daily basis, while diligently documenting the actions undertaken to achieve such improvement, one shall observe a gradual abandonment of any detrimental self-perceptions.

Engaging in literature and gaining knowledge from broadcasted documentaries, thereby acquiring education.

Engaging in crosswords puzzles facilitates the expansion of one's lexicon.

Engaging in cognitive exercises like Luminosity to enhance brain agility

Taking more time looking after yourself – thus enjoying self-development

Spending additional time with individuals who exhibit positive qualities is conducive to enhancing one's self-assurance.

Devoting additional time to the pleasurable endeavor of culinary experimentation is highly gratifying and can be shared and enjoyed with companions.

Prioritizing assistance to your loved ones or individuals in need inevitably fosters a higher sense of self-worth and cultivates positive thinking within oneself.

Indeed, as you come to recognize how your mindset and actions can influence the outcomes you experience, you also become aware of the extent of your control over your own life, surpassing any initial expectations. Furthermore, this will also enhance your self-assurance. It is imperative for you to progress in your life, and at times, it proves beneficial to set achievable objectives that bring you pleasure on a daily basis. Jot them down and ensure that they are endeavors that foster a positive sense of self. By adopting such an approach, you tilt the probabilities in your favor and consequently elevate the quality of your life, liberating yourself from the perpetual burden of feeling inadequate. You indeed meet the necessary standards, and it would be beneficial for you to disengage from any leisure time you may have been using to dwell on your unhappiness and hindered self-expression. By consciously selecting activities that promote personal growth, you are making a deliberate decision to engage in constructive endeavors that enhance your likelihood of attaining fulfillment and well-being.

One specific aspect in which I consistently fell short was allocating personal time for myself. I presently engage in this practice on a consistent basis, as it is imperative that individuals have equal opportunities to dedicate time to personal growth and the pursuit of life's pleasures. Upon recording and observing these percentages, it becomes apparent that a significant portion, namely 80 percent, of one's time is allocated towards negative activities, while efforts towards self-validation and positivity are insufficient. This revolves around the exploration of one's personal identity. Do not evaluate your self-worth based on the opinions of others, and cultivate the ability to refrain from harsh self-judgment. Life does not revolve around passing judgment; however, it does become inequitable when one leans towards insecurity rather than fully embracing every aspect of existence. Produce an illustration of the balance, adding the elements that elicit positive emotions or induce self-doubt in relation to one's self-worth, and it is highly likely that the equilibrium will be tilted in favor of the challenges and shortcomings. It is your responsibility to restore equilibrium and transition towards a markedly optimistic perspective on life and its treatment. There exist favorable aspects that can be pursued, and one must acknowledge that if their proficiency in a certain task is suboptimal, it may indicate that their aptitude lies elsewhere and they should consider exploring alternative paths or investing additional effort in honing the necessary skills. As you become more familiarized with that specific endeavor, your level of comfort increases, facilitating its execution.

Effective Practices To Cultivate A Positive Self-Image

What actions can I take to cultivate and enhance my self-esteem?

In order to enhance your self-esteem, it is imperative to confront and modify the detrimental beliefs that you hold regarding your own self. Though this task may seem formidable, there are numerous alternatives available that can assist you in its completion.

Engage in activities that bring you pleasure

Engaging in activities that bring you pleasure and allow you to showcase your skills can significantly contribute to the enhancement of your morale and the elevation of your self-esteem. This can be accomplished through the provision of incentives in the form of rewards in exchange for work performed, such as the provision of complimentary services, acts of care, or engaging in recreational activities.

Work

Employment can bestow individuals with aspects such as character, camaraderie, steadfast routine, and remuneration. Not many individuals thrive in a busy environment and value the opportunity to work towards their goals. Some individuals view work as an undesirable obligation or duty in the context of unpaid, volunteer positions. It is crucial that you maintain a sense of determination and support in your professional pursuits, ensuring that the balance between your work and personal life aligns with your own needs and satisfaction.

Pastime activities

This encompasses a wide range of activities, ranging from acquiring proficiency in a foreign language to engaging in vocal performances or enrolling in an art course. Reflect upon areas in which you perceive inherent qualities or endeavors that have aroused your interest for a considerable duration. Seek to explore exercises that offer moderate levels of challenge, enabling you to experience a sense of achievement and provide an avenue for nurturing your morale. The internet, public libraries, and adult education institutions should contain information regarding local clubs and classes that may be of interest to you. Engaging in the act of creating things contributes to a growing sense of self-affirmation within me. Upon observing my creation and finding favor with it, I consequently experience a sense of self-satisfaction, as it confirms my belief that I have unearthed a skill or talent within myself.

Endeavor to establish constructive interpersonal relationships

Make an effort to engage with individuals who are non-judgmental and with whom you feel comfortable discussing your emotions. By surrounding yourself with individuals who exhibit constructive and unwavering attributes, you are likely to experience an enhanced sense of self-esteem and increased motivation. Therefore, should you exhibit empathy and consistency towards others, it is inevitable that a favorable response will be elicited from them. This will allow you to cultivate a positive self-image and influence how others perceive you.

If one is afflicted by a lack of self-confidence, it is conceivable that there are individuals in close proximity who inadvertently reinforce the unfavorable beliefs and presumptions harbored by the individual. It is imperative to identify and address these individuals, potentially through bolstering self-assurance or employing constraints on the extent of engagement with them.

Discover effective strategies for asserting oneself.

Practicing assertiveness implies that you value both yourself and others and are able to communicate with mutual respect. It will aid you in establishing definitive boundaries. The subsequent elements will afford you the opportunity to comport yourself with greater assertiveness:

• Take into account your nonverbal cues in addition to the verbal expressions you use – strive to exhibit openness and confidence.

- Make an effort to articulate your emotions if they have been disrupted - refrain from speaking until you have regained composure, and then clearly articulate your feelings.

- Decline irrational solicitations. • Reject nonsensical solicitations. • Refuse unreasonable solicitations.

- Kindly communicate to others if you require extra time or assistance with challenging assignments.

- Endeavor to communicate using the first-person perspective when appropriate, for instance, "When addressing me in such a manner, I experience..." This provides you with the opportunity to express your needs in a manner that is neither assertive nor fearful.

Developing assertiveness can be a challenging skill to acquire, necessitating the need for practice through verbal self-reflection in front of a mirror or engaging in discussions with a trusted individual. Many adult educational institutions, such as schools and universities, also provide courses on assertiveness. Additionally, there are numerous self-improvement guides available for purchase or online utilization, offering practical exercises and tips.

Ensure the preservation of your physical welfare.

Caring for your physical well-being can enhance your sense of happiness and productivity, while also enhancing your mental self-perception.

Engaging in physical fitness activities enhances individuals' sense of well-being and self-perception. Engaging in physical activity releases endorphins, which are hormones known for their positive impact on mental well-being. This effect is particularly enhanced when exercising in an outdoor environment.

Rest

The lack of adequate rest can lead to an inaccurate representation of negative emotions and can result in diminished confidence, highlighting the importance of ensuring sufficient rest is obtained.

Diet

Consuming a nutritionally balanced diet during customary meal periods, alongside an ample intake of water and vegetables, will contribute to an enhanced state of well-being and overall contentment. Reducing or discontinuing your alcohol intake, as well as abstaining from tobacco and recreational drugs, can also contribute to the enhancement of your overall well-being.

Create a personal endeavor for yourself

When one establishes personal objectives and diligently strives to fulfill them, a sense of fulfillment and self-appreciation ensues upon reaching those targets, thereby engendering a growing sense of positivity and self-esteem.

Ensure that the test you set yourself is realistic and can be easily accomplished. It is not imperative for the matter to hold great magnitude, but it should possess significance to you. For example, you might opt to draft a letter to your community's newspaper or commence participation in a scheduled fitness program.

Devise strategies for identifying and questioning detrimental beliefs.

By cultivating a higher sense of self-worth, it is likely to unveil your underlying negative perceptions of yourself and their origins. This process may entail intricacies, thus it is crucial to allocate sufficient time while considering the possibility of seeking assistance from a companion or accomplice. If you are experiencing distress, it would be beneficial to seek guidance from a professional consultant in order to facilitate this process. It would prove beneficial to document notes, as well as any inquiries one may have. These, in turn, would assist in structuring one's thoughts.

- In your assessment, what are your areas of improvement or inadequacies?

- What negative perceptions do you believe other individuals hold towards you?

- In summary, if you were to provide a concise representation, what term would aptly describe your current state as an individual - 'I am...'?

- At what point did you commence experiencing these symptoms?

- Could you identify a specific encounter or event that might have led to this inclination?

- Have you observed a cumulative presence of persistent negative thoughts?

It may also prove beneficial to maintain a journal or log of ideas over an extended period of several weeks. Document the particulars of the circumstances, elucidate your emotional state, and articulate your perception of the fundamental belief or conviction that underlies the situation.

Concentrate on positive things. If one possesses a lack of self-confidence, it may necessitate substantial effort to acclimate and cultivate a mindset that fosters positive self-perception. One method of attaining this objective is to compile a concise inventory of attributes and qualities that you appreciate about yourself. "You have the option of including the following:

• Aspects pertaining to your personality

• Matters pertaining to one's physical appearance • Aspects related to one's visual presentation • Factors concerning personal grooming and appearance • Considerations regarding one's outward appearance

• Activities that you engage in • Actions that you undertake • Tasks that you perform • Behaviors that you exhibit • Pursuits that you partake in

- Developed skills you possess.

Please allocate an ample amount of time to discover and compile a list of 50 distinct items, without concern for the duration it may take. Retain this inventory and examine a distinct item from it on a daily basis. If you are experiencing negative emotions or high levels of stress in anticipation of an upcoming event, such as a job interview, you can employ this occasion as an opportunity to remind yourself of your positive attributes. If you encounter difficulty in generating a roster of valuable possessions, it may be prudent to solicit assistance from either an associate or a confidant in initiating the process.

Furthermore, this might aid you in perceiving how individuals could hold a more elevated perception of your worth than you do of yourself. An alternative approach involves documenting a minimum of three positive occurrences or achievements experienced on a given day prior to seeking rest. Several individuals also hold the belief that it is congenial to retain items, such as photographs or correspondence, that evoke feelings of self-affinity.

Engage in mindful practices

Mindfulness entails applying techniques such as meditation, controlled breathing, and yoga to center one's attention on the current moment. It has been demonstrated to facilitate heightened self-awareness by enabling individuals to better regulate their thoughts and emotions, thus minimizing their susceptibility to being overwhelmed by them.

Choosing The Right Company

Approximately a year ago, I gathered with my circle of acquaintances. It had been quite some time since our last reunion, and I always aimed to actively engage in their conversations, rather than solely focusing on my own interests. However, there were instances when I tended to dominate the discussion.

While enjoying beverages, I attentively listened to their conversation. I carefully listened to their discussion while partaking in refreshments. I partook in libations while simultaneously paying heed to their conversation. They were engaged in a discussion pertaining to mortgage arrangements and their respective occupations.

They were engaged in conversation pertaining to their romantic partnerships, betrothals, and maternal situations. While I was content for them, discussing topics that aligned with my interests, such as literature, self-improvement, my literary collection, coaching, or intellectual concepts, seemed somewhat incongruous.

Shortly thereafter, I encountered another cohort of acquaintances. They had served as cherished companions in my formative years, and we had shared many memorable experiences. Once more, I expressed the intention of inquiring about their interests, and despite their interest in my books, I remained unable to engage in a meaningful dialogue with them.

I experienced a similar sentiment to that of the other group when it came to discussing my reading material, personal objectives, and various other topics that I had delved into. It seemed that engaging in such conversations would not be suitable.

On a particular occasion, I engaged in a dialogue with an individual of utmost significance in my life. The person inquired regarding the temporal and financial resources I allocate toward my personal growth endeavors, expressing concerns over the associated risk involved. This occurrence instilled within me a sense of disappointment, and potentially provoked feelings of indignation. I made the conscious decision to discontinue discussing my personal growth interests with that individual, thus opting to remain silent.

Naturally, I remained in communication with them; however, I refrained from discussing those matters.

Subsequently, I commenced my participation in Toastmasters, where I engaged in coaching sessions and sought personal development within group settings. I discovered the individuals I encountered in that location to be highly approachable and receptive to conversation. I was able to lend an ear to them, and they reciprocated by attentively listening to me. I cultivated meaningful relationships that imbued me with a profound sense of vitality amidst the company of those individuals. I discovered that the same held true for my coaches and mentors; I was able to engage in discussions pertaining to my aspirations and strategies for progression with them.

It is highly likely that you can observe a prevailing activity occurring overhead.

I experienced a significant constraint on my vitality and overall wellbeing in the presence of certain individuals, whereas in the company of like-minded individuals, I thrived. It is imperative to acknowledge that there is no inherent issue with the mentioned groups of friends and individuals who hold a significant place in my life. However, it is apparent that they do not align with the same goals and their perspectives on life diverge, resulting in contrasting energies.

I am privileged to have largely escaped forming friendships with individuals of a negative disposition. However, there have been instances where I have encountered individuals who fail to comprehend my personal growth journey.

One observation I made while engaging in the learning process is that when I surrounded myself with individuals who were not able to comprehend the subject matter, it resulted in a sense of self-doubt. I have exercised discernment in avoiding the company of individuals with negative attitudes, as I acquired this insight at an early stage of my life.

In collective settings and personal development circles comprising individuals sharing similar attributes, I begin to experience a profound sense of well-being.

Therefore, the key takeaway lies in making prudent decisions regarding the individuals and environments one chooses to invest their time in. Individuals within one's immediate family circle and typically intimate acquaintances harbor a level of proximity that renders it challenging to simply elude their presence or sever the ties that bind. However, it is possible to engage in conversation by discussing shared interests.

It is advisable to refrain from engaging in conversations where there is a potential for disagreement, as this can lead to mutual agitation. Seek out reputable mentors, coaches, and online discussion forums where individuals share common interests. This will elevate you, enabling the expression of your authentic self. By refraining from expressing your true self, it may seem as though you are confined within the confines of a cage, thus exerting a detrimental influence on your self-esteem.

Action:

In the past year, I have engaged in an activity that has significantly impacted my life. It need not be prohibitively costly either. Navigate to a reputable online platform such as MeetUp, and peruse activities pertaining to your areas of interest, such as physical fitness, dietary well-being, personal growth, and vocal artistry. Subsequently, ascertain clusters comprised of those entities. Join one and attend. If this appears to be a significant matter, divide it into smaller components:

• Enumerate your areas of interest • Provide a catalog of your personal interests • Specify your preferences and hobbies • Outline the subjects that captivate your curiosity"

• Conduct a thorough investigation on MeetUp (or an alternative online platform).

• Examine the various groups and create a comprehensive listing of them.

• Please feel free to inquire for any additional information required.

• Please confirm your attendance.

- Participate in a singular occasion or gathering

- Subsequently, participate in an additional two.

In my opinion, the utilization of the rule of three proves to be advantageous when exploring fresh social circles. I engaged in this activity alongside my Toastmasters speaking cohort. Upon initially arriving, I found myself in the unfamiliar situation of not knowing anyone, a circumstance which caused my mind to generate the thought that this particular endeavor may not be suited to my needs or preferences. Subsequently, I fulfilled my commitment to attend the third event. In due course, I found myself delivering numerous speeches, cultivating new friendships, and thoroughly relishing the experience. I have assumed responsibility for facilitating and offering guidance in public speaking mentoring. Had I decided to quit after attempting it twice, this unfortunate event would not have transpired.

Self-worth refers to an individual's personal and affective assessment of their inherent value. It represents an individual's self-perception and self-evaluation. The amalgamation of one's self-perception and self-concept contributes to the formation of their self-esteem.

Certain sentiments that individuals experience in relation to themselves may encompass feelings of self-importance or self-reproach, triumph or defeat, elation or desolation. Certain convictions individuals hold about themselves may consist of statements such as: "I possess positive qualities", "I lack ability", "I deserve respect". Self-esteem, at its core, refers to one's personal evaluation and perception of oneself.

How is it developed?

The consensus among a majority of experts is that one's self-esteem can be shaped by various experiences endured throughout the entirety of their life, spanning from early childhood to adulthood. The level of self-esteem a child develops is significantly influenced by the role played by parents. If an individual experiences unwavering affection, their sense of self-worth will be fortified, and they will perceive themselves as esteemed and nurtured. Young children not only make academic comparisons with their classmates, but also assess themselves in terms of attire, conduct, and social engagements.

As the children mature, those who are fortunate to have responsible and nurturing adults in their lives who have established unequivocal limits and expectations exhibit the most robust level of self-assurance. During adolescence, the establishment of friendships and romantic relationships emerges as a significant contributor to the development of self-worth. Confidence serves as a reliable indicator of one's level of self-esteem. If your child possesses a strong sense of self-assurance and maintains steadfast companionships, it is probable that she possesses a strong foundation of self-worth.

What are the factors that hinder the establishment of a healthy self-esteem?

There are many things that happen in life that might interfere with the development of self-esteem and most of them happen in childhood. I have briefly addressed a few of these topics previously, and we will delve deeper into them in subsequent chapters. Numerous investigations have been conducted pertaining to the progression of self-esteem and the factors that hinder its advancement.

Research findings indicate that both genders equally experience and progress in the development of self-esteem without any discernible variations. Insufficient cognitive development, childhood health issues or disadvantaged socioeconomic background can exert influence on the formation of self-esteem at any stage of life. Stress, depressive tendencies, and Post Traumatic Stress Disorder (PTSD) collectively exert adverse effects on the cultivation of a robust sense of self-worth.

Dealing with Shame

Shame is among the primary factors contributing to low self-esteem. Embarrassment typically manifests in young individuals and may persist throughout one's lifetime, readily stimulated by seemingly arbitrary behaviors. Abandoned children develop feelings of shame as they mature, and similarly, children who possess distinctive qualities such as unusual height, lack thereof, excessive thinness or obesity, divergent skin color, or an inclination towards introversion can all potentially instigate this deep sense of shame.

When an individual, whether they be a child or an adult, experiences a sense of being devalued within the groups to which they are associated, it typically leads to the manifestation of shame. As a consequence, a reduction in self-regard transpires. In the event that your child faces exclusion from their peers during their time in junior and senior high school, it is probable that they may experience feelings of isolation and may potentially become the target of bullying. This leads to a significant decline in self-esteem and the emergence of self-doubt.

The Phenomenon of Bullying and the Adverse Effects of Diminished Self-Worth

As evidenced by frequent occurrences in our society, the act of bullying can have profound and deleterious effects on an individual's sense of self-worth, potentially leading them to contemplate or take their own life. Even after the individual ceases to be a target of bullying, the enduring impact on their self-esteem persists. Occasionally, there are overt manifestations on one's self-esteem, whereas in other instances, the repercussions remain concealed or suppressed.

Certain repercussions of bullying encompass a diminishment in self-assurance or the manifestation of self-questioning. The individual experiences a sense of inadequacy in some capacity. Self-reflection is an additional consequence stemming from bullying, as it leads to the internalization of the bully's remarks. This is particularly accurate when the act of bullying pertains to the physical attributes of the individual being victimized.

Several consequences of bullying can encompass:

- Nocturnal enuresis

- Social withdrawal

- The act of intentionally taking one's own life.

Summary and Action Plan

Self-worth is a pivotal and enigmatic facet of our inherent human nature, carrying immense significance that is often challenging to fully comprehend. It entails the introspective and affective assessment of an individual's personal value. Self-esteem encompasses the sentiments we experience towards ourselves and the convictions we hold about our own worth.

Action Plan

- Acquire knowledge about the theoretical construct of Abraham

Maslow's Hierarchy of Human Needs and the role of self-esteem within this framework; understand the significant impact of self-esteem on the psychological well-being of individuals.

https://en.wikipedia.org/wiki/Maslow%27s_hierarchy_of_needs

• Employ a diary to document each instance of experiencing shame and endeavor to discern the underlying cause that precipitated the emotion.

• Seek out an individual in your personal circle with whom you can confide your feelings and who is amenable to assisting you in identifying triggers.

Superlative Methods To Enhance Your Optimism

Seven Effective Strategies to Enhance Your Positivity

1. Surround Yourself with Optimistic Individuals

The individuals with whom you choose to associate wield a significant influence on your psychological state. It is widely acknowledged in the field of psychology that one's thoughts and behaviors are heavily influenced by the amalgamation of traits exhibited by the five individuals with whom they interact most frequently. These 'five individuals' may encompass actual individuals, such as those within one's social circle comprising of friends, family, and coworkers, or experienced influences derived from sources such as literature, television, online platforms, and printed media.

You exhibit a high level of cognitive openness. It acquires knowledge rapidly! These influences have the potential to either greatly benefit or severely jeopardize your well-being. If you consistently surround yourself with individuals of a negative disposition, your ability to experience happiness or confidence will invariably be impeded. Should one consistently associate with friends who frequently express dissatisfaction and grievance, it is likely that one would also adopt a similar disposition of constant complaint.

2. Engage with Literary Works, Visual Media, and Audio Recordings Produced by Esteemed Individuals

Recently, we deliberated upon the notion that it would be beneficial for us to allocate a majority of our time in the presence of individuals who exude positivity and possess a track record of achievement. However, in the event that there is a deficiency of individuals possessing such qualities within our present social network, what course of action should we pursue? What course of action should we pursue in this situation?

Here is some promising information - the exertion of positive influence does not necessarily require the physical presence of individuals. It could encompass their literary works, audio recordings, visual content, motion pictures, musical compositions... It all counts. Now you can no longer provide the justification of lacking resources to engage with those accomplished individuals.

Seek out individuals whom you hold in high regard and delve into their literary works, peruse their visual recordings, and tune into their auditory recordings... You will naturally assimilate their thoughts and actions.

Peruse their literary works, view their recorded visual content...

It is imperative to acknowledge that every aspect contributes to the transformation of our mindset into a positive one.

Proficiently written self-help literature and autobiographical accounts possess the potential to greatly assist individuals. An individual who has encountered numerous adversities throughout their lifetime resolves to compile all of their wisdom into a comprehensible book... This can be identified as a genuine prospect. You have the opportunity to acquire the knowledge and apply it in situations reminiscent of their experiences.

Engaging in literature enhances your creative thinking, broadens your intellectual horizons, and reveals the boundless possibilities that exist in our reality. Through the act of reading, one cultivates a fresh outlook on familiar matters, gaining insight into the diverse consequences that arise from varying courses of action. Books are beyond imagination. It resembles an expansive intricate network, wherein one continuously establishes connections between previously acquired knowledge and newly acquired information, thereby constructing novel solutions and responses.

As you persist in immersing yourself in favorable influences, you will ascertain an inclination toward harboring a higher frequency of constructive thoughts throughout the course of the day.

Regulating Key Emotions

The study of emotions has consistently surged in recent years. Numerous academic disciplines, including neuroscience, medicine, sociology, history, and computer science, have made noteworthy contributions to the development of theories that seek to delineate the nature of emotions and elucidate their origins. Ongoing research endeavors aim to examine the underlying factors that contribute to these emotional responses and explore their significance in an individual's experience.

Feelings can encompass a spectrum of positivity or negativity, often tied to a distinct pattern of physiological activity. They induce alterations in both the behavioral and physiological processes of an individual. According to the definition provided by the Oxford Dictionary, it can be stated that this emotional state is derived from an individual's specific circumstances, prevailing mood, and interactions with others. They can be described as the reactions we manifest in response to significant external and internal occurrences.

Emotions can manifest in four distinct forms: incidents, tendencies, transient, and enduring.

Psychologists affirm that emotions are experienced along a continuum of varying degrees of intensity. They possess a repertoire of typically synchronized reactions. The responses may manifest as behavioral, verbal, physiological, or neural mechanisms. Emotions may also be characterized as profound sentiments that individuals direct towards an object or an individual. In other respects, emotions can also be employed to indicate mild circumstances or convictions that are not specifically oriented towards any external object.

In a practical sense, Joseph LeDoux provides a definition of emotions as a result of conscious and cognitive processes that invariably manifest whenever the physiological system of the body responds to a stimulus. Conversely, psychologists delineate emotions as a complex variety of sensation that induces alterations in both physiological and psychological realms, thereby exerting an influence over an individual's cognition and conduct. Within the realm of social sciences, emotions are delineated based on their significant contributions to the cultural fabric of humanity and the myriad interactions individuals engage in on a daily basis.

Elements of an Emotional Experience
Klaus Rainer Scherer, an eminent scholar in psychology, originated the Scherer's component processing model of emotions, which delineates the five crucial constituents of an emotion. In order for the sensation to be recognized as an emotion, it is imperative that all the elements are harmoniously synchronized. Here is the chronological

sequence illustrating how the components are arranged during the occurrence of an emotional outburst.

Cognitive evaluation: This refers to the subjective perception and interpretation an individual forms regarding a stimulus present in their immediate environment. It entails elucidating how an individual's interpretation of an event shapes their perception of a given situation. It pertains to how an individual comprehends and promptly reacts to stimuli encountered during their lifetime. In general, it pertains to how individuals assess circumstances and entities in their lives.

Physical manifestations: These encompass the physiological elements that arise in the context of an emotional encounter.

Action tendencies refer to a crucial element that serves as a driver in the organization and guidance of an individual's motor responses.

Statement: Within the realm of emotions, an expression invariably corresponds to and accompanies an emotional reaction. They facilitate the conveyance of an individual's reactions and intended actions.

Emotions: These encompass the specific sensations an individual encounters when a state of emotional arousal arises.

Alterations in Emotional States
Modifications in Emotional Responses
Shifts in Emotional Dynamics
Transformations in Emotional Experiences

Emotional states invariably give rise to both internal and external transformations.

External modifications: These alterations refer to the discernible changes that manifest when an emotion is experienced. These factors encompass alterations in vocal tone, which aid in articulating the specific type of emotion being felt by an individual, modifications in facial demeanor wherein an observation of one's countenance may elucidate their emotional state, and variations in body language, including gestures made by the hands and legs, perspiration, furrowing of the forehead, or the erection of hair on the head, among others.

Endogenous transformations: These are the phenomena that are not immediately perceivable but consistently arise in response to a specific stimulus. The autonomic nervous system of a typical individual is comprised of two divisions. The autonomic nervous system, specifically the sympathetic division, assists in mobilizing the body's resources in response to a perceived emergency situation. In this scenario, an individual prepares themselves to either engage in combat or make a hasty exit from the current circumstances. The parasympathetic branch of the autonomic nervous system aids in replenishing the expended energy that an individual utilizes while evading or addressing a particular event. Certain physiological changes take place internally during an emotional state, including heightened heart rate, elevated blood sugar levels, rapid breathing, modulation of brain wave frequencies, pupil dilation, reduced saliva secretion resulting in a dry mouth, and diminished gastrointestinal functioning, thereby suppressing feelings of hunger.

The Benefits Associated With Possessing Self-Assurance

The majority of individuals can affirm that when one possesses confidence, they are inclined to obtain the greatest outcomes in life. Below are several ways in which the presence of confidence can lead to an increased sense of joy within your life.

#Enhances Performance

A deficiency in self-assurance can significantly hinder the realization of optimal performance. Can you reflect upon a specific occasion when apprehensions about potential failure deterred you from assuming a fresh responsibility? Now contemplate a coworker who willingly engaged in volunteering activities, driven by their steadfast belief in their competence to tackle any task, and their willingness to acquire new knowledge or enlist assistance from others whenever necessary. Your colleague likely performed exceptionally well, and as a result, might have received a salary increase or been assigned more significant and demanding responsibilities, thus gaining greater recognition within the organization.

What about you? What did you gain? Perplexity; languishing in the confines of an unprogressive occupation where your skills and knowledge remain stagnant, despite your unwavering belief in your capability, perhaps even surpassing that of your colleague. Your lack of self-assurance hindered your ability to surmount challenges and effectively apply your skills in order to achieve success.

#Increased Levels of Happiness

Individuals who possess a strong sense of self-assurance tend to exude a sense of contentment. You experience diminished concerns, a reduced level of anxiety, refrain from yielding to external influences, effectively articulate your needs, refrain from accepting compromises, and exhibit a decreased susceptibility to engage in detrimental competitions or becoming daunted by the achievements of others.

When an individual possesses a substantial level of self-assurance, they approach various situations in life with heightened vitality and resolve. This, in turn, leads to the cultivation of more significant interpersonal connections, the production of superior work, and a profound sense of interconnectedness with their environment. Furthermore, when possessing a sense of certainty in oneself, individuals are inclined to be influenced by one's actions, endorse one's choices, desire affiliation, and regard one as a role model, consequently reinforcing one's position in society as significant and purposeful.

#Better Health

"When one possesses a strong foundation of self-assurance and self-worth, they are endowed with enhanced capabilities to:

Mitigate adverse peer influence - as you do not exhibit a proclivity towards conforming with others in order to gain their approval or adhere to popular trends, you are less susceptible to engaging in irresponsible sexual behavior, gang involvement, and substance abuse. Consequently, you effectively circumvent all the associated health hazards associated with these activities.

Cultivate nourishing dietary practices - a deficiency in self-acceptance or self-love can diminish one's self-esteem and confidence, prompting the reliance on food as a means of emotional solace. This results in afflictions such as binge eating and bulimia, which have deleterious effects on your well-being.

Experience enhanced mental well-being - When one possesses confidence, one acknowledges mistakes and views them as inherent effects of the human experience. You embrace the notion that occasional errors are acceptable, as they are inherent to human nature, and proceed forward. Nevertheless, should you find yourself lacking in self-assurance, it is probable that you will magnify minor issues disproportionately. You engage in self-criticism, perceive pervasive evaluation and deeming of your shortcomings by others, and occasionally resort to drastic measures to conceal your mistakes. In general, individuals may experience a heightened state of stress, resulting in the onset of anxiety attacks, depressive symptoms, irrational apprehensions, the development of phobias, and a tendency to distance oneself from nurturing social bonds.

Emotional Stability

Self-assurance facilitates the attainment of a profound equilibrium originating from a genuine comprehension, embrace, and valuation of one's own being. You possess the capability of establishing objectives, successfully accomplishing them, and steadfastly adhering to virtuous principles. By adopting this approach, you effectively prevent yourself from sliding into the precarious territory of striving for approval and seeking acceptance. You abstain from eagerly pursuing validation and attention from others. You cease evaluating your self-worth based on others' opinions or considerations, or sacrificing your own needs to cater to their preferences. You prioritize your own well-being and embrace a beneficial level of self-care.

Less Self-sabotage

At times, we inadvertently assume the role of our own adversaries. Within our consciousness, there exists an extensive catalog of expectations, moral principles, and ideals that we feel compelled to adhere to, both mentally and occasionally documented. In our pursuit, we strive to achieve the standards that we have set for ourselves. My primary apprehension regarding these beliefs, values, and expectations pertains to their level of realism and reasonableness in terms of achievability.

In our pursuit of achievement, as per the standards set by our respective social collectives - including but not limited to familial, professional, religious, ethnic/racial, and similar associations - we inadvertently establish a paradigm dominated by expectations. For instance, consider the following statements: "I must attain the position of branch manager at a specific age... I must achieve a particular weight..." We exert ourselves to adhere to this catalogue of ideals, and when we fail, as we frequently do, our self-assurance plummets.

Nevertheless, in possessing self-assurance, one eschews such perfectionism and adheres to feasible benchmarks that are predominantly influenced by one's abilities and perspective on life. You endeavor to improve yourself, not in comparison to others, nor in imitation of others.

#Enjoy Happier Relationships

One tends to experience greater happiness when imbued with feelings of confidence and self-assurance, consequently fostering a natural affinity for others who exude happiness and confidence. Due to your reduced dependency (less reliance on reassurance, acceptance, affirmation), you become a more amenable individual to connect with, to spend time with, to coexist with." You demonstrate a commendable level of emotional resilience, enabling you to approach issues with a balanced perspective. As a result, instances of overreaction, disagreements, and conflicts are significantly reduced.

An individual who possesses confidence tends to demonstrate a propensity for being generous and giving within a relationship. Thus, the act of establishing a connection with you does not impose emotional or practical burdens on the other party, as you sincerely reciprocate emotions, willingly extend assistance and generosity, and display greater reliability and resourcefulness. People are much more likely to desire your presence. Having a strong sense of self-assurance is exceptionally appealing.

#Social Ease

Individuals who possess a strong sense of self-assurance exhibit charming traits that instill a sense of calmness in others and facilitate a seamless and effortless exchange of ideas, even in unfamiliar social encounters. These attributes comprise the capacity to actively engage in attentive listening, refrain from interrupting ongoing dialogues, maintain appropriate levels of direct eye contact, possess an understanding of when and how to communicate effectively, offer forthright and genuine compliments, refrain from excessively criticizing, and refrain from demeaning others.

Why? This is due to the fact that when one possesses confidence, their attention is not solely directed towards themselves, but rather towards others. Attending to others fosters a sense of importance, worth, intrigue, and contentment within them. Individuals who possess a sense of self-assurance also display a propensity for optimism and exude enthusiasm when contemplating future prospects. This is evident in the manner they conduct themselves, traverse, communicate, or articulate their thoughts. They emanate a formidable aura of optimism that is infectious and alluring to those around them.

Upon witnessing the myriad advantages associated with exuding confidence, as well as recognizing the potential hindrances that arise from lacking confidence, the subsequent endeavor involves acquiring the knowledge and skills necessary to cultivate unparalleled levels of self-assurance. I intend to impart extensive knowledge and practical guidance to enable you to revolutionize your life permanently, through the provision of 20 effective strategies. Prior to delving into that topic, it is paramount that we familiarize ourselves with the factors that led to the gradual decline of our previously thriving self-assurance.

www.ingramcontent.com/pod-product-compliance
Lightning Source LLC
Chambersburg PA
CBHW050255120526
44590CB00016B/2359